BMX

TRIX & TECHNIQUES

FOR THE PARK & STREET

TONY DONALDSON

MBI

To my loving wife and family, who encourage me to follow my dreams.

First published in 2004 by MBI, an imprint of MBI Publishing Company, Galtier Plaza, Suite 200, 380 Jackson Street, St. Paul, MN 55101-3885 USA

ISBN 0-7603-1963-4

Printed in China

On the title page:
Dave Mirra slides a front peg across the coping at the X Games in San Francisco.

On the back cover:
Stephen Scheurer does a Half hiker, a simpler variation of the Hitchhiker.

Tabletops are not always flat and crossed up. Mike Day hits a new-school version.

About the Author: Veteran rider and photographer Tony Donaldson's photography has appeared in the likes of *ESPN the Magazine* and *Sports Illustrated for Kids*, and in print advertisements for several top shoe, clothing, and bicycle companies. An avid mountain biker, BMXer, and skateboarder, Donaldson also works in the realm of digital video and is the co-author of MBI's *The World of BMX*. He lives in the Los Angeles area.

Author Tony Donaldson, age 16, at a local track in Illinois. *Madelyn Donaldson*

CONTENTS

FOREWORD BY TODD ANDERSON   6

PREFACE   7

ACKNOWLEDGMENTS   8

INTRODUCTION   9

CHAPTER 1: **GETTING STARTED**   11

CHAPTER 2: **FREESTYLE BASICS**   17

CHAPTER 3: **PARK & STREET RIDING**   31

CHAPTER 4: **FLATLAND**   55

CHAPTER 5: **DIRT JUMPING**   91

CHAPTER 6: **VERT**   113

INDEX   126

FOREWORD

So you want to learn how to freestyle?

Today's riders have more opportunities than ever before. With all the TV coverage and video games, freestyle has become mainstream. Whether or not you were born to freestyle, you still have to start somewhere, and this book is a great start. I remember trying to learn how to wheelie when I was 8 years old. I had to pull so hard to get that front wheel up, but I eventually got it. Why? Because it was FUN! I couldn't just ride my bike straight; I had to swerve, spin, jump, etc. etc. Now over 25 years later, I still can't go anywhere without spinning, jumping, or pulling a wheelie as far as I can. And it's just as fun as when I was 8 years old.

But what is freestyle? I think the definition varies from rider to rider. But I say freestyle is freedom to express your own personal style, meaning no rules. You're free to do whatever your imagination can think up. Don't worry about what everyone else is doing. Ride the way you want to ride. Do the tricks that you enjoy doing. Do your own thing. You never know who might follow your lead.

Whether you're going for a triple tailwhip, barspin, double backflip, or just trying to get up a curb, go for it, because it's FUN. Do it for the pure enjoyment. That's what riding is all about.

So here is a handy reference for all the cool tricks. Remember to always use your powers for good not evil. Now, GO RIDE!!

— Todd Anderson

PREFACE

I was approached by Dennis Pernu of MBI Publishing to write this book after working with him and J. P. Partland on another BMX book, *The World of BMX*. Actually, Dennis asked me to write two books on BMX, one on racing and one on freestyle BMX, simultaneously. Writing these books has been a good test of my 20-plus years in the sport as a racer, freestyler, photographer, and writer.

Freestyle was my favorite form of expression throughout my teen years. It kept me out of trouble and gave me a purpose. I think it will do the same for you once you get started. Freestyle is not easy; it takes a lot of practice. Learn the basics in the following pages, practice them over and over, and learn other tricks of your own design. Don't follow the crowd; rather, use your skills to create your own, unique stuff. There are no compulsory moves in freestyle, and copying everyone else certainly isn't *free*style.

Thanks for taking the time to read this book, and I wish for you to reap the same lifetime of rewards and fulfillment that I have from the great sport of BMX freestyle!

ACKNOWLEDGMENTS

BMX is my favorite sport. I grew up racing and having my own freestyle team, then worked for *BMX Plus!* magazine in the late 1980s. Thanks to mentor and former *BMX Plus!* editor John Ker for taking a chance on a kid from Illinois, and to my first mentor, Seth Perlman, who took me under his wing and taught me how to shoot.

Freestyle is a very individualized sport, hence the name. But among freestylers regardless of discipline there's a respect and brotherhood of fellow riders. This book couldn't have been completed without the help of many friends and fellow freestylers.

Thanks a ton to Todd Anderson, a hero of mine from the days when he was on the General Freestyle Team with legendary R. L. Osborn. Todd set new standards for blasting high airs and big style, and he was kind enough to show everyone how to get started riding vert in Chapter 6. He knows everyone in vert riding past and present, and most freestylers.

Thanks to Bubba Harris and Mike Day, not only two of the fastest racers on the planet, but also two guys who can definitely make the basics of dirt jumping look good. To Kyle Huber, visiting from out of town to ride street when everyone else was busy, his mastery of good park and street riding shows in the last photos I'll ever get to shoot at the Northridge Skatepark. Many thanks to Kanan and the crew there as well. Stephen "Hollywood" Scheurer was my flatland rider. Semi-underground but very devoted, he runs events locally just for fun and rides for the joy of riding. Scheurer came to me indirectly through my longtime friend Mike Drolet, whom I met when he had a green Mohawk and a helmet cut out to fit over it. No shortage of personality or talent in Mikey. You'll see him ride a little in Chapter 2 on freestyle basics.

I must also thank my wife, Jennifer, for giving me the time to write this book. It's one of two BMX books written simultaneously, and it's a bit different than writing magazine articles, my second job after providing photography to a lot of different outlets. Thanks also to my parents for encouraging me and driving me to races every weekend to, as my mom jokes, "Watch the mud dry." Mom also gave me encouragement to be creative, helped nurture my curiosity, and taught me how to do research.

Many thanks to MBI Publishing Company for the resources, assignment, and encouragement to write the books!

INTRODUCTION

BMX freestyle started as an offshoot of BMX racing. Kids had to do something between races. A few riders excelled in dirt jumping, like Trashcan Morgan and Harry Leary. Then a couple of riders started doing something else, not on dirt. Bob Haro, who started as a racer and progressed to making number plates and ultimately clothing and bikes, created a whole new sport by doing ground tricks and adapting a lot of elements, including skateboard-like moves and aerials at skateparks and wooden ramps. He soon partnered with R. L. Osborn, son of *BMX Action* magazine's publisher Bob Osborn, and the two brought the sport to the world via demos, the magazine, and more.

The sport exploded in the 1980s, and we soon had tons of amazing riders and people started specializing—guys like Mike Dominguez, Brian Blyther, Dennis McCoy, and newcomer Mat Hoffman on vert; Gary Pollak, Kevin Jones, Woody Itson, and Martin Aparijo on flatland; Pete Augustin, Dave Voelker, and Craig Grasso on street; Chris Moeller and Tim Hall on dirt, just to name a scant few. So many heroes from those days inspired the Mirras and Nyquists and Meyers of today.

Mat Hoffman alone kept the sport alive through the lean years in the early 1990s with competitions and dedication to making the best bikes for the best bikers. I should also mention that he showed the world what was possible on vert and dirt with backflips, flairs, 900s, and more. Hoffman's series became the BMX portion of the X Games from the start—nothing like having the best in the business running your BMX program, and competing in it.

Today the sport is accessible through games like Mat Hoffman's Pro BMX and BMX XXX, on ESPN and ABC via the X Games; through other specialized shows on less-mainstream cable channels; and at events near you.

Freestyle is a form of expression. It is a lifestyle. Riding your bike is not a simple hobby. It is a passion that consumes your every breath; you'd rather ride than anything else. It's intoxicating, it's addictive, it's . . . freestyle.

Rock star Cory "Nasty" Nastazio backflips in front of the Hollywood reservoir for a commercial.

CHAPTER 1
GETTING STARTED

BMX freestyle is one of the most fun things there is to do. You can do it anywhere—in the street, at a skatepark, on dirt, even in your basement.

Freestyle is about freedom of expression, and it's not a team sport, so you can really be yourself. If you watch the videos, read the magazines, and watch other riders, you can do what they do or do something completely different. The most creative riders make the best riders. You can specialize in one thing like Dave Mirra riding vert, or you can do several of the disciplines well like Ryan Nyquist.

There are four different "sub-sports" in the BMX freestyle world—flatland, dirt, park and street, and vert.

Flatland freestyle is one of the most subtle— riders doing insane spins and crawling all over their bikes. The best of the best have been doing it for years and practice eight hours a day, every day. They do things so smoothly and with such precision that an untrained observer never fully appreciates the amazing tricks they do. You'll hear fellow pros gasp at times when spectators don't get the big deal.

Trevor Meyer really pushes the limits of the sport. He's invented a lot of tricks that everyone else has had to learn after the fact. Martti Kuoppa goes home to Finland for months to learn new tricks and new routines, and he comes back with stuff nobody in the States has ever imagined.

Flatland bikes usually have all four pegs, usually large ones to give plenty of leverage for throwing the bike around. These bikes typically have small front sprockets for really low gearing, which makes it easy to pedal out of a trick. Weight is not a concern on these bikes, since they rarely leave the ground. Most parking lots or smoothly paved surfaces are good for flatland.

Dirt jumping is a sport that's easy to get into. Nearly everyone has access to dirt. Almost everywhere there's a trail that someone has built jumps on. If not, you can always go to a local BMX track to ride or see how they're built. At the trails, you can often find locals who'll help you learn to be a better jumper.

In Chapter 5 we'll get into the basics to send you on your way to jumping and throwing incredible tricks. BMX magazines feature photos of the latest tricks with how-tos by great riders such as Cory Nastazio, TJ Lavin, and Ryan Nyquist.

Park and street freestyle uses either man-made objects (think "urban jungle") like rails, planters, and angled walls, or specially built ramps and rails like you would find at a skatepark. Skateparks are becoming more and requirements and downloadable waivers for your parents to sign.

Street riding is fun. You just ride along and use various obstacles as part of your individual expression. Curbs and planters are everywhere. You can blast down a set of steps or do a 180 off a curb. Park riding is similar, but there are wood and cement obstacles and much better transitions between obstacles. You can blast air, stall on a peg or wheel, and grind across metal coping. It's up to you and your imagination, with a little bit of physics thrown in.

The fourth type of freestyle BMX is vert riding. There are elements of vert in park and street riding, but most vert riding is done on a halfpipe, quarterpipe, or in a pool. Most pools are better oriented toward skateboards because of their sharper transitions, but there are some skateparks with pools that are perfect for skateboards and bikes.

A big halfpipe may be intimidating, but remember: the bigger the ramp, the softer the landing if you're on the transition. It's like a big slide with a wood-like (Skatelite or Masonite) surface. Don't worry about the size until you're blasting big airs way over the coping (the edge at the top of the ramp, usually a metal pipe), at which time you'll think of the ramp as your friend.

Finding skateparks and other places to ride is easy, and if you decide to get into competition, there are listings in the magazines. *Transworld BMX*, *BMX Plus!*, and *Ride* all list contests in their pages and sometimes on their websites. *Ride* and *Transworld BMX* can be found online at www.BMXonline.com. *BMX Plus!* can be found at www.bmxplusmag.com.

One competition that has entries for beginners and pros is Core Tour, which you can find at www.thecoretour.com. Their competitions are bicoastal (New York and L.A.), so if you're nearby it's fairly easy. Elsewhere you may have to do some looking. Sometimes bike shops will know of local competitions.

Dave Mirra goes upside down and no-footed on the street course at the X Games.

more common. You can find the closest one online by checking www.SkateboardDirectory.com and going to the website of your local skatepark from there. Some websites include the hours, prices, and when BMX is safe there, as well as pad

Trevor Meyer shows the San Diego X Games crowd how incredible flatland can really be.

CHOOSING A BIKE

If you have a bike already, there's no need to read this section. If you don't have one, here are some things to consider.

If your friends all have bikes and love a specific brand, then that may be your choice. You might want to pick your own and be different.

After all, freestyle really is about individuality. Brand favorites come and go, and the best part is that most of the manufacturers know how to make bikes that ride extremely well. If you want, pick up some of the magazines and read up on what's out there. Most of them produce a buyer's guide every year, filled to the brim with the best information on the latest bikes and gear. Reading up on that stuff is half the fun!

When you're ready to buy your first bike, find a bike shop near you that specializes in BMX. You may not find one that specializes in freestyle, but the shop will at least have general freestyle bikes that you can customize.

Unless you're going into flatland *only*, you need a really strong bike with strong parts. Some riders like to custom order every part, but focus on things specific to your needs. Except for dirt riding, you'll need pegs on at least one side of your bike (forks and rear dropouts). You want a frame that won't break or bend easily. The best are usually 100 percent chromoly (all tubes) and fairly heavy because they're thick and reinforced for abuse. If you find that you bend or break forks a lot, one of the best brands is S&M's Pitchforks. Chris Moeller, the guy who designed them, really knows from a rider's point of view how to make strong forks.

Wheels, no matter what, are almost always 48-spoke and made for high-pressure tires and tubes. These days, most have 14mm axles so they're *really* hard to bend. Seats are usually small and padded, and the current trend is to keep your bars fairly narrow for easy barspins. You can cut stock bars down yourself or have a bike shop do it.

Stock bikes often come with one-piece cranks. Three-piece chromoly cranks are stiffer and stronger than one-piece ones, and they're also much more expensive and heavier. If you get a bike that's too heavy, you won't want to ride it as much. With heavier bikes it's harder to get as much air and whip around when you want to. It's a challenge to set up a bike that's strong enough but not too heavy. One of the best things to do is shoot for lighter and then replace with heavier as you bend or break things.

Check your bike at least once each day you ride for cracks in the frame, forks, bars, stem, and cranks. A minute or two a day can keep you from getting really hurt. Make it routine, either right before you start or right before you put your bike away.

When you first get home with a new bike, it will probably have all the CPSC-required (Consumer Product Safety Commission) stuff. This includes reflectors, a chain guard, and often a kickstand. The chain guard and kickstand are the first things to go. Your mom will likely complain about the reflectors, but you'll break them off if you don't remove them. And, unless you go overboard and put tons of them on for a specific look, reflectors don't look so hot. Yeah, they're safer if you ride at night, yada, yada . . . but really, take them off.

SAFETY GEAR

After you get a bike, you really should get some pads. Gloves will protect your hands because you're going to fall; knee pads and shin guards (get the neoprene ones, not soccer guards) will save your legs. Knee pads can also save your jeans if you wear 'em on the outside. Elbow pads are a good idea, too.

Flat, soft-soled athletic shoes work fine. Your favorite rider may have a brand you like, or you can be your own rider and get something else. Soft, flat soles grip pedals and pegs better.

Ramp riders usually wear full-face helmets; everybody else wears open-face, Pro-tec-style helmets. It really pays to invest in a good helmet. Bell Sports had a great marketing campaign years ago that said "If you have a $10 head, buy a $10 helmet." It's marketing, but it's also very true. You can beat up any other part of your body, but if you rattle your head enough, you'll have nothing inside it but a bunch of useless mush.

Check out the latest styles and talk to the people at the bike shop. Find one that fits comfortably, is made for what you're doing (you don't need a

Dennis McCoy does a "flair"—a backflip with a half twist—on the halfpipe.

motorcycle helmet), and gives you a full field of view. Full-face helmets—the ones with the mouth guard molded into them—are good for high-impact situations (such as ramps and huge jumps).

No matter what, it's good to have and use a helmet. And having your own saves you from getting to the skatepark and renting a helmet that's been used by 50 other sweaty riders. You can personalize your helmet with stickers from your favorite companies. Eddie Fiola used to use his sponsors' stickers to make an outside-the-helmet Mohawk.

Gloves protect your hands in a fall and help keep your sweaty palms from slipping off your grips. Many manufacturers make relatively inexpensive gloves, such as Pryme's "Trailhands" gloves that sell for about $16. Try several types and see which ones feel best on your hands.

Sponsorship is another area that becomes an obsession among many riders. The top experts and pros have sponsors, so *everyone* wants to be sponsored. How great would it be if you had someone who would fly you to competitions, give you free bikes and gear, and in some cases *pay* you to ride? It's every kid's dream. It can happen if you have the raw determination to be that competitive, but you have to be really committed and ride for years to get there. In the meantime, have fun. If you start getting good and winning contests, you'll get noticed. Martti Kuoppa started with an outside sponsor (in his case, an art gallery in Finland). He'd won gold medals before having a bike factory sponsor.

Not everybody has a cheerleading section when they ride, but very few people do a superman this well.

CHAPTER 2
FREESTYLE BASICS

Welcome to the amazing world of freestyle BMX, where you can express yourself in any way you like. To get going in any discipline of freestyle BMX, there are a couple of things you need to know. A lot of this information will cross over from one style to another.

The four main disciplines of freestyle are park and street, flatland, dirt jumping, and vert (half-pipe). We'll cover these in detail soon, but first let's cover some basic skills.

BUNNYHOP

RIDER: MIKE DROLET

The first thing you *have* to learn is the bunny-hop, whether you want to freestyle, race, or just ride well with your buddies down the street. You use this basic skill heavily in park and street riding, dirt jumping, and a little in vert. Though it is possible to do flatland without ever learning to bunnyhop, it's still an important skill. Put on your pads and helmet (it's all fun and games 'til somebody loses an eye) and get started.

TECHNIQUE

Start slow and low. Stand up, pedals level. Pick a crack in the street or a small twig for reference. You need a goal and a crack may be easiest. Start off riding along and pulling the front wheel off the ground. Yeah, it's a wheelie of sorts, but you're not pedaling yet. So it's more of a "manual"—a non-pedaling wheelie. Get comfortable doing that in a straight line. Be careful you don't pull up too hard or you'll loop out and wind up on your butt. Trust me, it hurts!

If you're having trouble, make sure your handlebars are straight up and down from the stem. If they're too far forward or too far back, you won't have good leverage. If you can't reach any other way and your bars are way back, you need a shorter stem or shorter frame. The opposite is true if you have the bars way forward. Either of the two extremes of handlebar placement looks stupid and will make everything harder.

When you have the front wheel wired, go after the same crack, just let the front wheel roll across and lift your back wheel. "What?!?" you say. Crouch down a bit and push forward on your bars as you unweight your feet on your pedals (sort of a hop, but your feet never leave the pedals). Though it is possible to flip over the bars this way, you'd have to be trying to do it. You don't have to try to roll distance with this; it's just getting you used to the motion.

Ready for the next part? It's time to get both wheels airborne. It's fun—three-dimensional (sorta) freedom.

Try a twig for reference this time. If you don't make it over, or if you hit it on the way up, it's easy to tell. You'll feel and hear the twig snap as you hit it, and the twig will snap instead of causing you to lose control. Approach slowly. With the pedals level, crouch down to preload your body to spring upward. It's kind of like jumping while holding the handlebars and keeping your feet on the pedals. At first, you just want to pull both wheels up at once and get over the twig.

The secret to truly great bunnyhops is to pull up hard, keep your feet level, tuck your butt well behind the seat, and try to stretch out and touch your seat to your chest. This body position pulls the bike up much higher. When coming back down, pull up on the bars slightly to drop the rear wheel first. You want it to hit just before the front to help you absorb the landing. Let your body relax and crouch into the landing. Your body will absorb some of the impact and it will be easier on your bike. You can also correct slightly if you get a little crooked in the air.

Once you can pull both wheels up and over the twig, try to do it with the front wheel first. You can go much higher this way, starting your hop by pulling your front wheel way up and springing off your back wheel. The record for height on this maneuver is nearly 50 inches. That's over 4 feet between the bottom of the tires and the ground! Height isn't what we're going for yet, though. You have to build up skills and strength. You want to level out at the apex to let yourself go over the obstacle.

001-007

To learn bunnyhops, start slowly with just one object as a reference. Use a twig or a 2x4 or a cardboard box, something that won't hurt you if you land on it.

Once you can pull up front wheel first, then back wheel, over a twig without breaking it, use two twigs. Keep moving them farther and farther apart. This may take a few days, and your arms will be *sore* if you've never done this before. Don't overdo it; you can hurt yourself if you overtrain.

When you can get the twigs a few feet apart, try hopping over taller things. Collapsible things like cardboard boxes (e.g., cereal boxes) are great for this. Work your way up to leaving the box perfect as you bunnyhop over it on the tallest side. Curbs will be no problem for you when you can bunnyhop over a cereal box. You can have contests with friends on these. If you get really into it, you can build a stand with nails in it every couple of inches and set a flexible bar across it to keep track of your progress (like a limbo bar).

008-013

When you master bunnyhopping one object, start building your skills with two objects spaced farther and farther apart. This will give you plenty of confidence when you're hopping up curbs and over random toys and will keep you from having to replace so many rims.

010

011

ENDOES

RIDER: MIKE DROLET

The "endo," derived from "end over end" crashes, is another good first skill. It'll give you an idea of the balance point of your bike for everything from rolling flatland tricks to crazy toothpicks and other lip tricks on ramps.

The object is to learn these slowly and with a lot of control. You can get hurt if you don't work your way up. As you become more skilled as a rider, you will learn how to get out of a bad situation carefully, and that takes practice. When you practice, you'll make mistakes. How you handle those mistakes directly relates to how fast you'll improve.

CURB ENDO

The curb endo can be done without brakes. Approach a curb slowly—slower than you'd walk. A good endo can be done by barely moving. It uses almost all body motion and only a little contact with the curb. You want to crouch on the approach, with your weight slightly back. Lightly

014-025

Start out doing the curb endo really slowly. Use more arm and body motion than speed to lift up the back of the bike, keep your arms extended fully at the top and tuck your body back, and see how long you can hold the bike at the balance point.

"kiss" the curb with your front tire, throw your weight forward a little to unweight the back wheel, then push hard with your arms to pivot the bike over the front axle. As the bike goes up, tuck back and feel for the balance point. See how long you can hold it. If you go too far and the bike starts to flip over, step down onto the curb. If the flip is further along, step *over* the bars and onto the curb.

There are a lot of things you can do from here: take off a foot, or when you get really good, both feet (you'll sit on the seat at the apex for this one). These variations are old school, but good for really wiring the balance on the front wheel.

To get out of an endo, let the back wheel come down slowly, keeping your knees bent with your arms outstretched, slightly straightening your legs on the way down. As when you touch your front wheel to the curb, come down *slowly*. Shift your weight back quickly, pulling back (not up!) to start a backward roll to pull away from the curb. Pedal backward a foot or two, then pedal forward to push off and ride forward, turning sharply away from the curb as you do this.

BRAKE ENDO

A front brake endo is essentially a curb endo without a curb. It'll teach you to throw your bike up just the right amount for front wheel rolling tricks and peg stalls. You'll learn good balance by mastering the front brake endo. Of course, you can't do it without a front brake.

As with the curb endo, go slow. Crouch with your weight back a bit. Lock your front wheel as you unweight the back end of the bike. Push forward on your bars and straighten your arms as you tuck back. Practice going up to the balance point and try to hold it for a while.

This is virtually the same as a curb endo, with some cool advantages—you can steer into it and snap your hips the same direction, and if you do this into the balance point, you can spin 360s on the front wheel. You can also go up straight and x-up the bars (turn them 180 degrees as you go up, your arms will have to bend for this), do one- and no-footers, and expand from there. Have fun with it, and pedal while you're balancing (forward or backward). Another fun old-school trick is a front wheel hop. You have to really settle into the balance point and use your body to hop the front wheel up and down (about an inch).

To get out of a brake endo, do the same as you did to get out of a curb endo. You don't have to roll backward since there's no curb to avoid, but it's a good style point to roll back a little.

026-033

The brake endo is just like a curb endo without the curb. Make sure your brakes will fully lock the front wheel, then just ride up slowly and lock them as you push forward with your arms. Hold as long as you can. The peak is where you can take off a foot or two or get into other variations.

029
030

032

033

Ryan Nyquist can ride anywhere from vert to dirt to parks and do it better than almost anyone else. Here he barspins his way through the Vans skatepark in Ontario, California.

CHAPTER 3
PARK & STREET RIDING

Skatepark riding and street riding are similar. Skatepark riding is easier, safer, and offers more stuff to ride and trick on in a smaller area. And, fortunately, communities are discovering that it's safer to have a good place for kids to ride, and more individual cities and private enterprise are building parks. City-owned parks are cement and *free*, where privately owned parks usually have wooden ramps and a small fee to ride.

Street riding offers urban terrain—including planters, handrails, and concrete transitions. It also has dangerous vehicle and pedestrian traffic to contend with. In many communities, street riding is considered destructive and dangerous, so it's illegal. You could be chased by anyone from business owners to security guards to the police. Be aware of the local laws and be kind to the business owners and security guys, and often you'll be allowed to ride in fun areas much longer.

One of the first things you have to know to be able to ride these types of obstacles is how to bunnyhop. (See Chapter 2 on freestyle basics and start learning the bunnyhop.) It's the foundation for just about everything on your bike, and it'll help you keep out of trouble if one of your buddies lands in front of you.

You'll need to have a set of axle pegs; it's your choice whether to have front and rear on one side or both. Axle pegs do add weight, but they can help you to use both sides of the bike. A helmet is a *really* good idea for street riding since there are all kinds of hard objects around to smash your head on. You're likely to fall and slide your hands across a variety of surfaces and gloves will keep your hands from getting cut up, which would prevent you from riding.

I recommend buying and using every pad you can at first, especially if you aren't confident in your abilities. Many kids don't use pads, but some skateparks require helmets and other pads. If you want to cut back on what pads you use, make sure you know what you're doing. Be smart—you should push yourself to learn new stuff, but don't ride over your head. That said, let's get down to the fun stuff!

MANUALS

RIDER: **KYLE HUBER**

Manuals are wheelies without pedaling. They are a good way to link tricks and they just plain look cool. You can practice manuals at any speed, though slower often requires more balance than faster ones.

Start out learning manuals on the ground. Ride along, pull up on your bars to pull up your front wheel and lean *way* back; work on being able to hold that as you roll along. If you start to loop out (fall backward), you can feather your rear brake a little to drop your front end a bit, and lean back or give a little pedal to bring the front end up. For the most part, whichever foot you normally ride with forward should be up and the other one down to help keep your weight way back.

If you have to, find cracks in the ground and practice holding the front end up between them. Then find cracks or marks farther and farther apart. When you have those wired, work on learning to bunnyhop into a manual. This will allow you to bunnyhop up onto a box or ramp deck, manual across it, and drop back in. As you approach the box, bunnyhop a little earlier than you think you need to. This sets you up with your front end a little higher and makes landing in a manual easier. You may hit the edge and pop a few tires as you're learning; this will happen if you're short on landing your back tire on your obstacle.

When you're finished with the manual, you can just drop your front end, but it's also a great thing to learn to bunnyhop out of it. For example, you can learn to bunnyhop onto a planter, then hop over a small gap and immediately into another manual, or just bunnyhop off. The combination of manuals and bunnyhops gives you options and far more control. And bunnyhopping a little earlier than you might expect helps you keep the front end up if you need it to keep a manual going.

001-008
Practice manuals on the ground before you try doing them over big boxes like Kyle Huber does.

007

008

009

010

009-016

Bunnyhopping into a manual isn't as easy as it looks. You'll need a lot of practice with manuals to perfect this.

RIDER: **KYLE HUBER**

If you want to build your confidence on ramps and park courses, peg drop-ins are for you. They're also useful in getting down from peg stalls.

Start on the deck of the ramp, set your bike's pegs on the coping, and set your pedal against the coping. If your bike is resting on the right pegs, your right pedal should be back and resting on the coping. Step your right foot onto your right pedal and swing your left foot over and onto the left pedal and balance there, keeping your weight on your right foot.

Look at your front wheel. When you're ready to go, turn your front wheel to the left (down the ramp) as you lean your weight in toward your left side a little to help pull you off the coping. If you're leaned back as you do this, you risk slipping sideways and sliding on your hip down the ramp. As your front wheel comes off, lean with the turn and roll down the ramp. Your bike should just naturally roll down; your rear peg will unhook itself and your rear wheel will roll down behind you.

Before you approach the ramp, make sure you're carving the ramp, or turning and moving across, to the right side for your pegs. Ride up as far to that side as you can, so if you drift a bit when you carve, you can still stay on the ramp's coping.

As your front wheel approaches the top of the rail, make sure the peg lands on the coping and push your bike into the coping (while leaning your butt out). Your body should lean a little over the transition of the ramp to allow you to be ready to come back into the ramp. If your body is too far over the bike or biased over the deck, you'll likely get stuck and possibly fall onto the deck.

Hold it there and balance for a second or two, keeping your pedals level. As you get better at this, you can go up a little faster and slide across the coping. Of course, at that point you're no longer doing a peg stall; it's now a rail slide.

To get out of the stall and drop back down the

017-025
Peg stalls are another good basic skill. Taking a foot off at the top when you're first learning can help you learn proper speed and timing.

ramp, lean your body away from the deck as you turn the front wheel toward the bottom of the ramp. Your front peg will drop off the coping and your front wheel will pull back down the transition and start rolling down the ramp. Your back wheel has no choice but to follow. Ride down the transition and make sure you don't ride off the edge of the ramp.

The first time you try this on a ramp, you might want to first just ride up and put your foot onto the deck as your pegs get near the coping, just so you get a feel for it. As your pegs land on the rail, put your outside foot on the coping until you're confident you're at the right speed to comfortably set your pegs on the coping without taking your foot off to learn to balance your stall.

GRINDS

RIDER: **KYLE HUBER**

Grinds are easier to learn on a ledge than on a rail, and ledges offer more opportunities to get off the bike and out of danger if you're not on perfectly. For the best results, you may want to use smooth, deep pegs and wax the curbs, rails, coping, and ledges you ride. Candle wax works, as does the special wax you can buy at skate shops.

Going across the box, line up so that your front wheel isn't too far over before you bunnyhop. You don't want to smack your peg on the side as you go up. Make sure your front wheel goes up as you bunnyhop and lands right next to the edge so your peg locks on. Remember, the edge or rail you're jumping onto is on a downward slope, so you don't have to bunnyhop that high.

As your front peg goes up onto the ledge, your back peg should just follow through. Make sure your body is up over the ledge and lean the bike into it a little so you don't slip off the edge. With your balance over the ledge, you can control the bike easily if you need to go one way or the other. Keep your pedals level and your body relaxed.

When you get to the bottom of the ledge, pull up or bunnyhop slightly before you drop off the ledge, and lean back a little so your bike will be fairly level on landing. If you slide straight down a steep ledge, your front wheel will hit first and may throw you into the ground or damage your wheels or forks on a really hard hit.

026

027

026-033
Peg grinds are the same if you bunnyhop onto them or jump to them.

028

FEEBLE GRIND

RIDER: **KYLE HUBER**

You can put your front wheel and back peg on the ledge for what's called a "feeble grind." It's actually pretty controllable since you can steer and your wheel rolling makes you go faster.

034

035

034-042

Feeble grinds are a good skill and easy to control on a sloped rail or box.

036

RAILS

For rails it's much the same. As you approach, you'll bunnyhop right as your front peg passes the beginning of the rail, depending on how fast you're going. If you're going really fast, you can bunnyhop before the rail. If you're going walking speed or slower, wait until your front wheel gets past the start of the rail. Bunnyhop up, put your front peg on the rail, and let the rear peg follow and lock on as you're sliding.

Make sure your body is centered over the top of the rail. Keep your body relaxed and your knees bent. Coming off the rail is basically the same—you want to bunnyhop or at least lean your body back and pull up slightly to level off the wheels as you land. Bunnyhopping off gives you good control on small rails and is good practice for big rails and situations where just rolling off the rail would be dangerous.

ICE PICK STALL

RIDER: **KYLE HUBER**

An ice pick stall is a bunnyhop to back peg stall on a planter or coping or bench. It's a good next step to building more skills and it looks really cool, too!

Start off by rolling toward your object at a comfortable angle. The first photo here shows Kyle Huber coming in at 90 degrees. You can come in parallel as well. Come in nice and slow; you don't need much speed at all. Bunnyhop a little earlier than you think you have to, and land your rear peg on the edge of the planter or box. If you come in straight at the wall, you have to bunnyhop and turn 90 degrees in the air. Pull up high and hard—you have to bunnyhop enough to get your rear peg onto the object and have your front wheel up high enough to let you hit the balance point. The higher the front wheel, the better.

Center your body weight over the ledge as your rear wheel locks on. If your front wheel drops, it'll either land on the ground and your back peg will drop off, or your front peg will land on the ledge as well and you have a double peg stall. Your front wheel might land on top, in which case you can always step off and start over.

While you're stalled in the ice pick, you want to have your front wheel slightly over the ground, not the ledge. This makes getting out of it easier. When you're learning this, you can just let the front wheel land on the ground and let your back peg slide off. Once you get that down, learn to bunnyhop off for more options and control. When you start doing ice pick stalls on ramps, you can go faster and the stall can become a grind. The basic idea and where your weight is centered are the same.

043

043-051
Ice picks are impressive-looking on a planter or box.

044

045

046

047

44

BUNNYHOP 180

RIDER: **KYLE HUBER**

The bunnyhop 180 is much like a regular bunny-hop with a twist. It's a good skill to learn on the ground and work up to ramps.

Start off going at a moderate pace. As you begin your bunnyhop, steer slightly in the direction of your spin. Turn your head and shoulders around and bring your body with it. When you first start on these, you'll go about 90 degrees. Keep working on it until you can get a full 180 degrees. As you're first learning the bunnyhop 180, start from almost no speed.

As you get to where you can do the first 180, when you land use either your brakes or forward pedal pressure to bring up the front wheel a little

and swing the bike around for another 180 to get you moving forward again. Landing and going backward is really tough unless you have either a coaster brake or free coaster, because with a free wheel you have to sit down and pedal backward as you roll that way. If you want, you can even bunnyhop almost 360 degrees, land on your back wheel, and finish whatever part of the 360 you haven't hit. Brakes are useful here, but just putting pressure on your forward pedal to keep your pedals level and your wheel from moving works well and helps keep your momentum since you're already on the pedal and ready to get moving.

052-060

Bunnyhop 180s are a good thing to learn on the ground to open up crazier tricks, like 180s to backward grinds. Another variation adds a 270- to 360-degree bunnyhop. Forward pedal pressure or brakes can help you swing the bike around on the back wheel to finish.

054

055

059

060

SMALL RAMP AIR

RIDER: **KYLE HUBER**

You can put that bunnyhop 180 to work for small ramp air. Approach the ramp with enough speed to get air—in other words, to go higher than the coping on the ramp. You can start out by just carving below the coping and working your way up. As you get more comfortable with air, you can go higher and higher. If you're going to carve or air to the left, you want to be at the far right side of the ramp on the flat bottom. When you go up the ramp, start to turn (carve) in the direction you want to go.

Watch your front wheel as you go up. Pull up and back toward you a little as it leaves the surface so you don't run into the deck. As you arc and start coming back down, spot your front wheel and make sure it lands in the top part of the transition. Make sure your back wheel doesn't hang up on the coping. Tapping your brakes a little in the air can help bring you back over the coping so you don't hang up.

The closer to the top of the transition you are and the smoother you can land, the more speed

061

061-067
Small ramp airs are fun tricks to do at small halfpipes at skateparks and will prepare you for the bigger ones.

you can build as you pump the ramp. Landing too close to the bottom takes away all your speed and also makes for a much harsher landing.

Pumping the ramp is a semi-natural skill. Push down with your legs and arms at the bottom of the transition after each landing. As you get to the other side, use your legs and arms to help you spring up and pull yourself up the transition. In a halfpipe, even a small one, this can help you build a *lot* of momentum, certainly a lot more than if you tried pedaling. This is how guys like Mat Hoffman, Jamie Bestwick, and Dave Mirra blast 8- to 10-foot airs over a big halfpipe.

066

067

Arguably one of the best flatland riders of all time, Trevor Meyer shows San Diego what he's made of. He can string together basic and advanced tricks like nobody else.

CHAPTER 4
FLATLAND

RIDER: **STEPHEN SCHEURER**

PEG WHEELIE

Stephen says you need no brakes for this one. Step onto your back left peg with your left foot. Pull up the front wheel with your arms to the balance point, so it's not falling forward and you're not looping out. Use your right foot to balance by moving it to counterbalance the bike. You want to keep your arms stiff while you hold the bars so that all the balance is controlled by your right foot.

When your arms get tired or you're just done with the trick, let the front end come down, put your feet back on the pedals, and ride off. If you do have brakes, you can tap the rear brake to help you drop the front end, though it's smoother by just using your leg.

This is the trick you'll really learn balance on, and this is the balance you'll need for all other tricks.

001-008

Peg wheelies are the foundation of modern flatland riding. Master these and everything else will fall into place.

005

006

007

008

57

MEGA SPIN

RIDER: **MIKE DROLET**

Stephen says no brakes for this one either.

Ride along normally at a slow pace, then step onto your back left peg with your left foot. Start by turning your bars to the right so you're heading in a circle. Halfway into your circle, pull up on the bars like you're going into a peg wheelie. As you pull up on the bars, pulling the bike into you tighter, you'll start to spin on the back wheel in a tight spin, and your back wheel will stop spinning and actually start to go backward.

As the wheel starts to go backward, kick it backward with your right foot. Keep kicking the tire in short kicks repeatedly without letting up. This will keep the momentum of the spin going. You control the spin with the kicks. Keep your arms stiff.

To get out of the spin, give the tire a hard kick that will force the wheel to turbine forward again; then set the bars down and ride off.

009–017

Mega spins will get you used to scuffing and spinning, and they're just plain fun.

009

010

011

012

013

014

015

016

017

60

FIRE HYDRANT

For this one you will need brakes.

Ride along at a normal pace, step onto the back left peg with your right foot and the front left peg with your left foot. Put all your weight onto your left foot, and push yourself into your handlebars in a clockwise manner using your right foot. You will swing around 180 degrees clockwise while standing on the front peg.

As soon as the 180-degree swing is complete, pull up gently on your handlebars. This will cause the bike frame to start to swing back toward you as the wheel comes up. When the frame gets about a quarter of the way around, tap your brakes and catch the top tube of the frame with your right foot.

Step onto your pedal with your left foot and ride away.

018-025

Fire hydrants take awhile to learn but are another really good part of a flatland trick foundation.

FUNKY CHICKEN

This one needs brakes as well.

Ride along at a normal pace, step onto the back left peg with your right foot and the front left peg with your left foot. Put all your weight onto your left foot, and push yourself into your handlebars in a clockwise manner using your right foot. You will swing around 180 degrees clockwise while standing on the front peg.

As soon as the 180 is complete, grab the seat with your right hand and press the brakes with your left hand. This will cause you to do an endo on your front wheel. While you're doing a mini-endo, swing your right leg over the handlebars and start scuffing the tire forward. Scuffing is when you kick the tire forward, drag your foot along the tire backward, then kick the tire forward again. This allows you to control the tire, and the bike as well.

The key is to never stop scuffing or you'll lose control. Be sure to hold your seat and handlebars securely, and use their positioning to balance the bike.

To ride out, throw the frame under your right leg in a clockwise manner. Then set the back wheel to the ground and kick forward. After kicking forward, pull your right leg back through the handlebars and pedal away.

026-034
The funky chicken is a great way to learn one-wheeled balance and scuffing.

026

027

028

029

030

031

032

STEAM ROLLER

Stephen says no brakes are required for this trick.

Ride along at a normal pace, step onto the back left peg with your right foot and the front left peg with your left foot. Put all your weight onto your left foot. Kick the back end of the bike around in a counterclockwise manner. When the frame reaches 180 degrees, catch the seat with your right hand. Hold your seat and your handlebars securely, and use their positioning as well as the movement of your right foot to balance the trick.

To ride out, throw the frame back toward you in a clockwise manner, and step to the back left peg with your right foot and pedal away.

035-043

Steam rollers will get you gliding your way to one-wheeled mastery.

038

041

043

WHIPLASH

No brakes on this trick.

Ride along at a normal pace, step onto the back left peg with your right foot and the front left peg with your left foot. Put all your weight onto your left foot. Kick the back end of the bike around in a counterclockwise manner. When the frame reaches 180 degrees, step to the front right peg with your right foot.

Lift your left foot from the front left peg, and use it to catch the top tube of the frame when it comes around to a 360-degree point. Step to the pedals with your right foot and pedal away.

044

045

046

047

048

049

050

051

70

HANG FIVE

No brakes are needed for this one.

Ride along normally. Step to the back right peg with your right foot and the front left peg with your left foot. Put all your body weight on your left foot. Push the handlebars forward so that you do an endo, and take your right foot off the back peg. When the seat of the bike reaches you, straighten your arms so that it stays against you.

Keep your arms secure to keep the back wheel up in the air, and use your right foot to balance by moving it to counterbalance the needs of the trick.

To ride out, just let go of the security in your arms, let the back end fall down, and pedal away.

052-059
Hang five

KARL KRUISER

No brakes needed for this one.

Ride along at a normal pace, step onto the back left peg with your right foot and the front left peg with your left foot. Put all your weight onto your left foot. Push the handlebars forward so that you do an endo, and take your right foot off the back peg. When the seat of the bike reaches the hang five position, use your right hand to grab it.

The key to this trick is to lock your arms so that the handlebars and the frame are securely positioned. Use the positioning of the seat and handlebars as well as the movement of your right foot to balance the trick.

To ride out, use your right hand to throw the back wheel to the ground and then grab the handlebar with your right hand and pedal away.

060-068
Karl kruiser

You'll need brakes for this one.

Ride along at a normal pace, step onto the back left peg with your right foot and the front left peg with your left foot. Put all your weight onto your left foot. Grab the seat with your right hand, and press the front brakes with your left hand. As soon as you endo, put your right leg between your left leg and the forks, and start scuffing the tire. Use the positioning of the seat and handlebars as well as the scuffing movement of your right foot to balance the trick. The key is to never stop scuffing or you will lose your balance.

To ride out, throw the frame around 180 degrees in a counterclockwise manner and kick the front tire while setting the back wheel to the ground. Then step to the front left peg with your right foot, and the back right peg with your left foot. Put all your weight on your left foot, and use your right hand to grab the left handlebar, and your left hand to grab the right handlebar, and then pedal away with your bars backward.

069-073
K Squeaks

069

070

071

PINKY SQUEAKS

Brakes are needed on this trick.

Ride along at a normal pace, step onto the back left peg with your right foot and the front left peg with your left foot. Put all your weight onto your left foot. Press the front brake with your left hand and kick the frame counterclockwise with your right foot. As soon as the frame reaches 360 degrees, step over it with your left foot and put your left foot back on the front left peg. Then use your right foot to kick the front tire backward once before the frame swings under your right foot.

After you kick the tire backward and the frame swings under you, press the front brakes again and let the frame swing around again. The key to this trick is to control the momentum by kicking the tire at the right time and for the right distance when the frame comes around.

To ride out, just catch the top tube with your left foot, set the back wheel down to the ground, and pedal away.

074-082
Pinky Squeaks

HALF HIKER

This simpler variation on a trick called the "hitch-hiker" requires no brakes.

Ride along at a normal pace, step onto the back left peg with your right foot and the front left peg with your left foot. Put all your weight onto your left foot. When in the Karl kruiser position, put your right foot on the front right peg, and take your left hand off the handlebar. The key to this trick is to keep your front wheel level between your two feet, keep your right arm locked securely on the seat, and use your left arm and your body to balance the trick.

To ride out, grab the left front handlebar with your left hand and throw the bike back to the ground with your right hand. Then step to the back left peg with your right foot, grab the front right handlebar with your right hand, and pedal away.

083-090
Half hiker

084

083

085

086

090

HALF PACKER

No brakes needed for this variation of the "back packer."

Ride along normally. Step to the back right peg with your right foot and the front left peg with your left foot. Put all your body weight on your left foot. Push the handlebars forward so that you do an endo, and take your right foot off the back peg. When the seat of the bike reaches you, straighten your arms so that it stays against you. You'll be doing a hang five at this point.

While doing a hang five, put your right foot on the front right peg and grab the seat behind you with your left hand. Let go of the handlebar with your right hand. Keep your left arm locked securely on the seat, and use your right arm and your body to balance. When you have this balance under control, swing your right leg over the handlebars, and to the front right peg.

Now you are rolling in the half packer position, which is in front of the handlebars with both feet on the front pegs and holding the seat with your left hand. The key to this trick is to keep your front wheel level between your two feet, keep your left arm locked securely on the seat, and use your right arm and your body to balance the trick. To ride out, lean to the right and take your right foot off the front peg and do a K squeak.

Use the positioning of the seat and handlebars as well as the scuffing movement of your right foot to balance the trick. The key is to never stop scuffing or you will lose your balance.

To ride out, throw the frame around 180 degrees in a counterclockwise manner and kick the front tire while setting the back wheel to the ground. Then step to the front left peg with your right foot and the back right peg with your left foot. Put all your weight on your left foot, use your right hand to grab the left handlebar and your left hand to grab the right handlebar, and then pedal away with your bars backward.

091-099
Half packer

091

092

093

094

095

096

097

098

099

Bubba Harris is not only one of the fastest racers on the planet but also a stylish trail rider as well.

CHAPTER 5
DIRT JUMPING

Dirt jumping started as an offshoot of racing. Riders would go out and see how much air they could get, and naturally they were after style as well. It started off with simple cross-ups and one-handers or one-footers, and progressed to tabletops, 360s, and more.

In the 1980s, a guy from Phoenix, Arizona, named Jose Yanez did the first backflips, starting by jumping into a river and later making a special ramp. Yanez was featured in the movie *Rad* doing the stunt riding for Cru Jones whenever he did a backflip and also worked for a time for the Ringling Bros. and Barnum & Bailey circus. He was the only rider for several years who did backflips since they were considered so dangerous.

Now backflips are considered an intermediate trick and riders do crazy variations like throwing tailwhips or barspins in the middle. There are even a couple of riders—like Dave Mirra—who now do *double* backflips—crazy stuff.

But if you're just starting to get into jumping, you won't be doing double backflips, at least not in the next week. First, you have to get the basics.

Find some small jumps to try and begin with single jumps. Most areas have BMX trails with a variety of small jumps. Start out small and get a feel for jumping them, getting a little air and landing with your back wheel first. Keep your arms and legs loose and relaxed to absorb the impact of the landing.

When you're comfortable with that, find a small double jump. Make sure it's not the kind that has a pit dug in the middle to build the two jumps; it's best to start with two small rollers.

If you aren't sure you can make it across both, you can try the 50/50 method. Approach at moderate speed and jump it. If you land a little short, have your front wheel fairly high up and your body relaxed, legs bent. You want to make sure the front wheel clears the top of the second double. Your front wheel will come down right after the back wheel hits. As long as it makes it over the jump and you're relaxed, you'll make it. This is the way to land short without crashing.

Keep trying to jump a little farther until you can clear the double comfortably. Then start trying the other doubles on the track or trails, working your way up to the biggest ones. Don't jump anything you're not comfortable jumping; work your way up slowly and within your own ability. Crashing on the bigger jumps is dangerous, and dirt can be nearly as hard and unforgiving as cement.

If you land straddling the crest of the second jump (called "casing" the jump), most trail jumps are soft enough to absorb the majority of the landing and let your body absorb the rest. Keep your feet on the pedals if you can, just don't fall backward into the dip between the jumps or go over the bars. Your sprocket will get dirty and you'll have to use your legs to absorb what the jump can't, but you'll be lighter on your body for it.

Once you have doubles down and are comfortable and consistent enough to get air and have enough hang time to throw some tricks, you should learn to pump the jumps. Pull up on the front of the jump, throw your trick, and land smooth enough on the back side to push down hard and gain speed before doing the same on the next jump. Land just past the crest of the jump so you have plenty of back side to ride down to minimize the impact. If you go too far, you'll flat bottom, i.e., land too far, past the jump and lose all your momentum. If at all possible,

your bike should be angled almost the same as the landing so your back wheel touches down a split second before your front. If you find yourself coming down with your weight too far back or your front wheel too high, lightly tap your rear brake to drop the front end. There are a few people who ride with no brakes, and they have nastier accidents as a rule. Bubba Harris has great technique on this from years of riding some of the best trails in the country. When you see his technique, you'll understand how he was ranked number three in his first year as a pro.

If you have to bail, it's best to let go of the bike so you can run or slide down the back side of the jump. Keep your arms and legs loose—keeping them stiff is the surest way to get hurt.

You can learn pumping just by doing or by riding halfpipes or even BMX tracks. Halfpipes allow you to gauge how well you're pumping by how much higher you get on each side of the ramp without pedaling.

001-008
Wiring the basic jump will give you the skills and hang time to move up to the crazier stuff.

001

VARIATIONS

RIDER: **BUBBA HARRIS**

CROSS-UP

This is a great way to get your first venture into style. These are so easy that some riders do 'em while racing. Go up just like a basic jump, and in the middle you turn your bars 90 degrees to the side. A little lean on the bike in the same direction as you're turning the bars adds more style.

009-016

A cross-up is one of the first things you learn once you get the basic jump down.

014

016

017-024
The x-up takes the cross-up to a whole new level.

017

018

RIDER: **BUBBA HARRIS**

X-UP

This one's a cross-up on steroids. Go up just like a basic jump, lean back a bit, and keep your legs a little straighter than you would for a normal jump. You have to leave room for your bars to clear your knees when you turn them. Twist your bars all the way around. The name comes from the X your arms form as you turn the bars at least 180 degrees (Bubba Harris and his rubber arms can go about 270 degrees). Unwind your arms and ride away happy. You can practice and warm up for these on the ground, just turn your bars around as far as they'll go with you still attached.

019

020

021

RIDER: **MIKE DAY**

NO-HANDER

When you take off, pull the bars up toward your body. For old-school style, pull the bars all the way to your hips. Hold the bike with the inside of your legs and hold your hands up and out as far as you can. Holding them straight behind you is a variation called a "suicide." Hold it as long as you're frozen in the air, then get your hands back on the bars and reorient the bike down the landing jump.

You might want to start by taking off one hand first, extending it as far as you can. Eventually you'll be comfortable enough to get it off and back on and feel that you have full control of the bike. This is one way to learn "switch-handers," where you take one hand off and move the other hand to the other side of the bars (e.g., take off your right hand and extend it out, then grab the right grip with your left hand).

025-032

Mike Day shows how big a no-hander can be.

RIDER: **MIKE DAY**

TABLETOP

To do a "tabletop," leave the jump with good control of your bike. Bring one arm in toward your body, extend the other one, and crank the bike as hard as you can. Use your legs to bend up and pull the bike up on its side as flat as possible. Use your body, your legs, and your feet on the pedals to help pull up the bike. It will help if you take off with your back leg set as the bottom-side foot on the bike. Your back foot then pushes against the crank arm and that leg pushes the bike from underneath.

Old-school style is to turn the bars so that the front wheel points straight up and the bike is completely flat on its side. New-school style just tweaks the bike flat or past flat and has the bars pointed straight ahead with the bike's direction, drifting the table as far as possible. You can do variations on this, like spinning the bars around 360 degrees while throwing the table or taking your lower leg off and extending it the opposite direction. Really good riders can do both, and I guarantee they can also walk and chew gum at the same time. It takes a lot of skill, coordination, and practice!

To get out, use your top leg and your arms to bring the bike back to its original upright position and drop the front wheel to get ready for a soft touchdown on the upper back side of the landing.

033-040

Tabletops don't always have to be flat and crossed up. Mike hits a new-school version.

034

035

036

037

RIDER: **BUBBA HARRIS**

TURNDOWNS

As you take off from the jump, start to kick out the back of the bike and spin your cranks about halfway so you can reach around the bike for maximum tweakage. Once your bike is sideways, you want to lean in and crank it around while you crank the handlebars 180 degrees in the opposite direction of your kickout. The farther past 180 degrees you get the bars, the cooler this one looks. Just make sure you don't get your bars hooked on your leg—it's not good if you can't reverse your turndown.

Getting out of a turndown is easy—straightening out your bars helps you twist the bike back to its normal position for landing. Come in smoothly just past the top of the landing jump.

041-048
Turndowns look best when fully clicked and held for as long as possible.

045

047

048

049

050

RIDER: **MIKE DAY**

UN-TURNDOWNS

The un-turndown is technically quite a bit different and more difficult than the turndown. Get airborne with the front end basically straight up, keeping the bars pointed straight up the same as the bike. Use your body and your legs to pull the bike hard to one side. As shown by super jumper Mike Day, you can get extra style points for crossing up the bars just a bit—and for going as huge as he does.

To get out of it, use your legs and arms to bring the bike back around and level it off before landing. Absorb the landing with your arms and legs and be prepared to be cheered by adoring fans as you ride away.

"The Condor" Mat Hoffman is one of the all-time best riders and bike makers, and is probably single-handedly responsible for promoting and making freestyle riding what it is today.

CHAPTER 6
VERT

RIDER: **TODD ANDERSON**

Getting air is at the top of the thrill charts and is one of the most exciting aspects of freestyle BMX for riders and viewers alike.

Ramp accessibility depends a lot on your region. In some areas, there are skateparks close by, but for others the only option is to build their own ramp. Plans are available online if you're not sure how to build a ramp. Ask about skateparks at your bike shop or check out www.skatepark.com. Lots of cities are recognizing the value of having a safe place to ride, but call ahead to make sure they allow bikes.

Before you get going on vert, put on a helmet. Open face or full face, put one on. Ramps and skateparks generally have hard surfaces and sharp corners that can hurt you really badly. Don't ride beyond your abilities. Do push your limits, but be able to control the outcome if something goes wrong. The more padding you wear, the safer you'll be. 'Nuff said.

Todd Anderson says, "When you first start out, everybody has to do it just like their friends. That's wrong. If you're goofy [-footed] or if you're regular, don't worry about it. Do whatever is comfortable for you."

Whether you're regular or goofy depends on which foot and which pedal are back when you turn in the air. A person considered to be "regular" has his or her back foot on the inside (bottom) of the turn, and a person who is "goofy-footed" has his or her back foot on the outside (top) of the turn. For example, if you turn to the left with your left foot back and right foot forward as you turn in the air, you're "regular." Todd rides goofy and always has, and he stresses that though that riding style adds a little difficulty, every person should ride their own way, with his or her own style. As he'll tell you, that's why it's called *free*style.

No matter how fast you go up the ramp, at the peak you want to pull up and do a perfect 180-degree turn in the air before landing. That applies whether you're learning to do airs at the bottom or you're more advanced and flying well over the coping. Don't worry about carving across the ramp at this point, especially if you're not on a really wide ramp. You basically want to start off going up the middle of the ramp, turning in the air, and coming down the middle.

The most common problem for beginning vert riders is pulling up too early. If you don't pull up at the peak of your air, you won't get the most air. Pulling up too early can also send you too far into the ramp and your wheels will hang up if you go over the coping. The result is similar to pulling up too early in dirt jumping. Start low on the ramp and work your way up until you can consistently air smoothly.

001-008
Todd Anderson shows the basic air. You can start below the coping, but proper technique is the same whether you're above or below the coping.

009-016

Todd shows you how not to do an air. Taking off too early makes you land higher than you started—a bad idea if you go over the coping—and actually will get you less air.

014

015

016

PUMPING THE RAMP

On a quarterpipe, your speed is determined by how quickly you can pedal up to it. Staying smooth and pumping well on your way up will maximize your air. But on the halfpipe the pump makes all the difference in the world. Done right, like Hoffman or Dave Mirra or Jamie Bestwick, pumping the ramp means dropping in on one side and hitting a 6-foot air on the opposite side, almost effortlessly. Pumping takes *way* less energy and gets you a lot more air. Pedaling is *not* the best way to build speed and get air. The riders at the X Games have mastered pumping the ramp, and they're definitely worth watching.

Proper riding and pumping are easy once you learn how and practice a little. Whenever you land air, your tires should land as close to the top of the vert as possible without hanging up. Landing too far down near the flat bottom takes away all your speed and can really hurt or cause you to crash.

Once you've landed near the top, keep the bike close to you and push it down hard on the transition, pushing it away from your body and down toward the ground. This builds speed on the landing side of your air. When you approach the transition, crouch a little and use your body to pull yourself up the transition faster. As you get more air and good pump, you can easily redirect it a little for long carving tricks.

LOOKBACK

You've mastered airs over the coping. You can get several feet over the top. Now you need a challenge. The lookback is a basic trick, but one that looks really cool when done well and tweaked out. It's a way to push yourself to the next level so you can get into crazier stuff. Before you attempt a lookback, make sure you can consistently do solid airs well over the coping with plenty of hang time in the air.

When you start to get air, let your body hang back and push the bike up higher. "Throw the bike, and leave your body," Todd says. You're twisting your body against the bike, letting the bike twist away from you. You want your bars to either point the same way you went up the ramp, or a little opposite of your turn for style points. Hold it as long as you can at the peak of your air, then unwind the whole thing and complete your turn, landing at the top of the transition, riding off with a casual smile.

017-024
Lookbacks are a good old-school trick to learn. They look really great, and are in the runs of a lot of top riders.

017

024

023

A one-footed air, or even a one-handed air, is similar to a regular air. You want enough hang time in the air to comfortably take off a limb or two or three, stretching them out as far as you can. Get high enough over the ramp to hold your limbs out the whole time you're at the peak of the air.

Mat Hoffman started taking this trick to the next level early in his career. He liked to execute multiple tricks on one air. For example, he would go up, do a no-hander, then put his hands back on the bars and throw his feet off for a no-footer. You have to have a *lot* of hang time to pull this off. Mat can usually do two or three variations like this.

025-032

Taking off a hand or a foot or a couple of either is an essential skill once you have enough air time to comfortably do it.

029

030

031

032

INDEX

Anderson, Todd, 6, 113–125

Basic air, 114–118

Bike choices, 13, 14

BMX Plus!, 12

Brake endo, 27–29

Bunnyhop, 17–34

Bunnyhop 180, 46–50

Cranks, 14

Cross-up, 95–97

Curb endo, 24–27

Day, Mike, 101–105, 108–111

Dirt jumping, 11, 91–94

Drolet, Mike, 17–29, 58–60

Endoes, 24–27

Feeble grind, 41

Fire hydrant, 61, 62

Flatland bikes, 11, 14

Funky chicken, 63–65

Gloves, 15

Grinds, 39, 40

Half hiker, 82–85

Half packer, 86–89

Hang five, 71–73

Harris, Bubba, 90–100, 105–107

Helmet, 15

Hoffman, Mat, 112

Huber, Kyle, 32–53

Ice pick stall, 43–45

K squeaks, 76, 77

Karl kruiser, 73, 74, 75

Kuoppa, Martti, 11, 15

Lavin, TJ, 11

Lookback, 119–121

Manuals, 32–35

McCoy, Dennis, 15

Mega spin, 58–60

Meyer, Trevor, 11, 13, 54

Mirra, Dave, 11, 12, 91

Moeller, Chris, 14

Nastazio, Cory "Nasty," 10, 11

No-hander, 101–103

Nyquist, Ryan, 11, 30

One-footer, 122–125

Park riding, 12, 31

Peg drop-in, 36

Peg stalls, 36–38

Peg wheelie, 55–57

Pinky squeaks, 77–81

Rails, 42, 43

Ramp pumping, 119

Ride, 12

Safety gear, 14, 15

Scheurer, Stephen, 55–57, 61–89

Small ramp air, 50–53

Steam roller, 65–67

Street riding, 12, 31

Tabletop, 102–105

Transworld BMX, 12

Turndowns, 105–107

Un-turndowns, 108–111

Vert, 113

Vert riding, 12

Wheels, 14

Whiplash, 68–70

X-up, 98–100

Yanez, Jose, 91

The World of BMX
ISBN 0-7603-1543-4

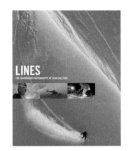

**Lines: The Snowboard
Photography of Sean Sullivan**
ISBN 0-7603-1678-3

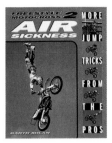

**Freeestyle Motocross II:
Air Sickness**
ISBN 0-7603-1184-6

Mountain Bike Madness
ISBN 0-7603-1440-3

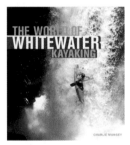

World of Whitewater Kayaking
ISBN 0-7603-1962-6

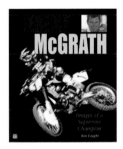

**Jeremy McGrath: Images of a
Supercross Champion**
ISBN 0-7603-2032-2

The Cars of Gran Turismo
ISBN 0-7603-1495-0

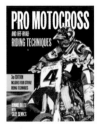

**Pro Motocross and Off-Road
Riding Techniques, 3rd Ed.**
ISBN 0-7603-1802-6

**The Cars of
*The Fast and the Furious***
ISBN 0-7603-1551-5

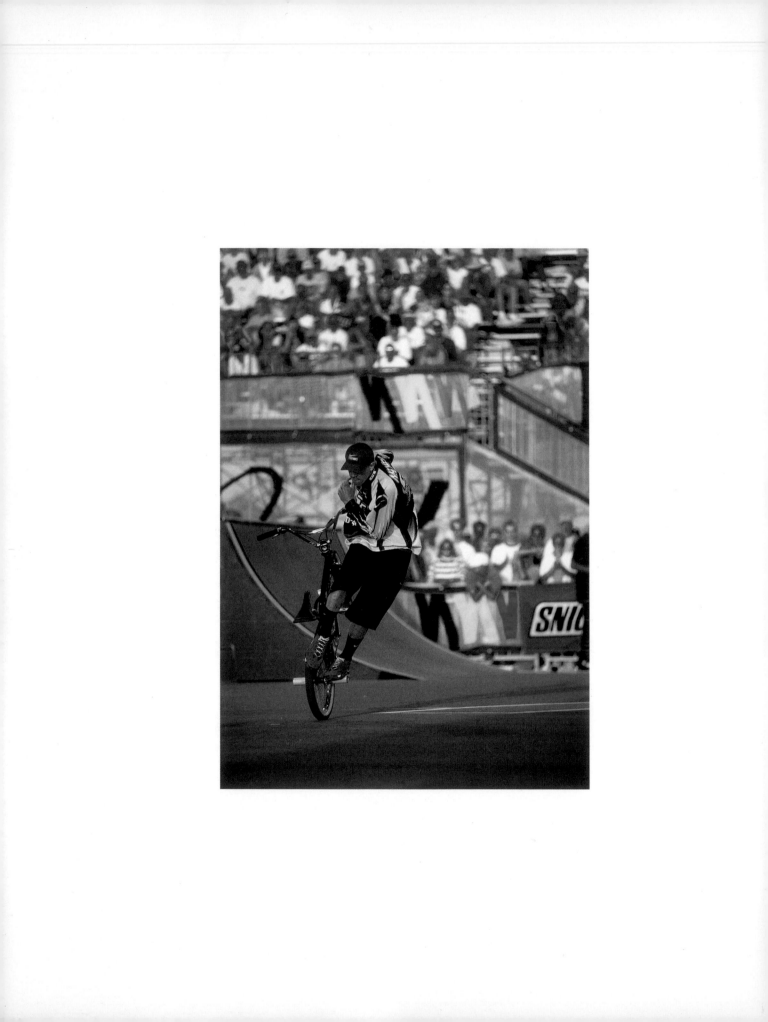